MW01273094

Astral Projections

"Above me I saw something I did not believe at first. Well above the haze layer of the earth's atmosphere were additional faint thin bands of blue, sharply etched against the dark sky. They hovered over the earth like a succession of halos. — *David G. Simons, first balloon ride above 100,000 feet.*

A Note from the Publishers

There are two kinds of space exploration. One: you do with physics. The other: you do with poetry. The best astronauts we know not only defy gravity with aerodynamics, but also defy gravity with words. And it gives us hope, that maybe we don't need 12,000 kilonewtons of sheer force to bolster humanity past the atmosphere and know the universe where we belong.

Good morning,

Good afternoon,

Good evening.

Welcome to our mission of space exploration.

(by Nikka Ursula)

The Dark Matter Within

We wish you a good flight. Everything is all right.

—*Sergei Korolev to Yuri Gagarin, the first man in space,*
after counting down to Vostok 1st lift off

Ouranophobia

by kam

i. when the sun didn't rise, we scrambled to explain. the tides came in and out, and clouds crossed the sky. there had to be a reason.

ii. the stars began to fall. they landed in our back yards, smoking hot and glittering. we didn't know why. they weren't the rocks we'd believed them to be. they were made of gold and silver. we poured water on them and brought them inside. they sang beneath our fingers. we couldn't measure them.

iii. the moon began to speak. it circled the globe slowly, whispering over our shoulders, telling us secrets we weren't meant to know. we stopped scrambling and listened. we were already lost.

iv. the sun came back, but it was too late. we knew.

you were my judgment day

by Riley Estrada (publisher)

ten billion people emerge to watch the earth end.

scientists say, this is it.

the ground quakes

with the force of

shaking human knees.

we move mountains one last time.

the radio said it would come in a flood.

the television told us the earthquakes

would kill us for sure.

my mother whispered,

before i slept,

that it was the asteroids,

the ceaseless army of asteroids,

that would mark up the earth

until it was as pale and gaunt as the moon.

they say today is the day
the sun will swell

and devour us whole

but you have already kissed me.

i have already been drowned.

i have already shaken

and i have already burned

I Only Want to Matter

by kam

when i was a star

and you an astronomer

you saw me

named me

made me your own

and i shined all the brighter for being yours

i loved you as a star loves a stargazer

a love born of seeing and being seen

of recognition

of import

and so i shone for you

until i could no longer

and who remembers a star burnt out?

YLEM

by Pallas Anders Pallisco

surrounded by the

s u p e r v o i d

lone coldspot

i enter each quantum

universe as if it were

my last entrance

my true name

transcend

z e i t g e i s t

i am surreal

i am singularly

put

i n t h e y l e m

sessile by inertia

to respond in urges

notwithstanding useless

i a m y l e m

whether dark in parka

or unyoked from moksa

defenseless at the kalpa

i a m y l e m

A Repressing Crowd of Angels

by Noah Jones

breathe in the air for me because I can't

bright but dark and suffocating, the stars squeeze me,

watching as they dance through each other like

french tips tapping on a foggy windowpane

pale blue grey lips trembling as they tug up at the corner

the elegant stretched fingers of mannerism alien,

beautiful, silver and glowing

and throwing away all that came before,

looking toward the future, already there,

waiting for me

waiting for us to catch up

breathe for me because I can't

neck stretched too far, too far back

eyes cast toward the darkness, lips open, screaming, quiet

as the planets swirl in the deafening distance

and I bury my nails in my sides and it burns like

acid rain hissing as it strikes the ground

a high ringing somewhere in the distance in this empty office

stage lights striking the tops of eyelashes in the right position comforting

and familiar, warm

but the eyelashes tremble and it's all you can see,

the only light in a dark room that could be stretching on forever,

blinding light, burning and staying for hours after as you sit, waiting,

waiting for sight

waiting for sight to catch up

(I still can't breathe)

Houston, I Think We've Had a Problem

by Nikka Ursula (publisher)

We bless the craters of the moon with names,

yet we are not allowed to honor

the marks on our body.

And so, I sanctify my own indentations:

      Abenezra, the flare of red across my forehead,

      Kastner, the remnants of wounds on my knees,

      Humboldt, the lines of my body stretching and growing,

      Bohr–the faded scars on my wrist.

There is no room here

for your footsteps,

or your flags.

I claim my own landscape.

To Love the Universe

by Andrea Bremner

There was once a time when you would look at the world in wonder,

Pondering the secrets of the cosmos.

It was as if the stars gave parts of themselves to you with every whisper,

For your eyes shone with the light of a million galaxies.

I am glad souls are hidden as I am certain yours is a supernova;

A celestial explosion so bright that the dark of the Moon dances under its

light,

And the Sun itself shields itself from your beauty.

A single glance at your brilliance would engulf me in a flame so sweet

I wouldn't dare complain.

Space Boy

by Holly Melling

you held galaxies in your hands.

blades cut on your thigh and you bled stars.

the beating of your heart sounded a lot like the birth of planets.

and you kissed the world goodbye, giving me only the moon to remember

you by.

you were the fabric of time and I swear when she left I could feel you

ripple.

your fingertips felt as hot as the sun.

the stares were as blinding as a solar eclipse.

and you kissed the world goodbye, giving me only the moon to remember

you by.

you still orbit around me.

if i look up i can see you enjoying yourself.

you're never coming back down.

so I still remember the moon.

i would burn just to be near you

Riley Estrada (publisher)

there is something about your palms.

if you asked the sky to weep

meteors would fall, screaming

thank you, thank you,

thank you.

For You

by Mendy Lu

the stardust gathered from my lungs to yours.

a piece of me,

a piece of the universe,

giftwrapped

and made solely for you

and your eyes.

the flecks of bluish purple green.

the hues that naturally came together

to create the colors of the nebula and galaxies

that are depicted in works of art

and inspires beings

such as us

to write about it.

you are the muse

that brings the jumbled mess together.

the one who orchestrated the trail of stars

so that when they fell,

it would create a painting engraved to be seen for centuries to come.

So please.

take these handful of stardust

and throw them back into the night sky.

So that I can become that painting,

that work of art,

to be engraved in the vast space

that is

your heart.

An Atom at Home

by Savannah Stoehr

Tonight, I remembered how

the stars wink down at me,

and my skin winks back.

I remembered how the breeze

passes through my shimmering bones –

breath; a lung far greater

than tissue can conceive.

I felt myself fading, feet sinking like roots

into the grassy earth beneath them, fingers

tangling in wisps of firmament.

I remembered that I am little more

than empty space

and light, and I forgot

how to be afraid.

what poets always tried

by Shristi Pant (publisher)

i think the night sky finally taught me

the words to explain love to myself :

love is like,

squinting at one pinpoint of light in the crowded sky

until all the others blink out.

or its like,

gazing so long that stars become

s t a r s and s t a r s and s t a r s.

Constellations.

by c. abad

I want to tell you about the times I tried to drown my fears in tears and I want to show you the stars that exist inside of your bones because your hands have seen many nights and survived all of their frights and I want to show you your life rattling in the wind like prayers strung on branches of flimsy trees. Your palms are a story, darling, and the lines on your face are a roadmap of empty promises and sinking sorrows that have carved their names in the roots of your soul.

You said to me once that the stars have loved me from the very beginning when everything was water and empires crumbling. Maybe before Iris caused trouble in Troy and maybe before I started bleeding ink out of my fingertips because I am trouble now, you said, I am the prayers rattling in God's mind that go unanswered, I am a reckoning force. They'll put you up in the sky when you die my little fire, you said, they'll put you up in the sky.

Let me tell you about the paths of your veins, about the composition of the gas that's inside of your heart. I want to talk science and logic but I'm the poetry within the hearts full of initials, you said, I'm the grooves of a record, I'm a storm in the ocean, I'm a bonfire in the forest, I don't know what kind of chaos connects everything that's lost, you

said. I remember you once told me they'll put you up in the sky when you

die my little fire, you once told me that stars loved the skin on my bones

and that the Gods have called me by name during the nights when they

searched for someone to save your soul, but no one really gets saved, I said.

No one really gets saved because we are the only ones who know exactly

how deep our roots go.

You were never going to be saved. I know this. I knew this when I tried to

kiss your wounds closed and your tears only fell like autumn leaves

because you may have lights in your bones, but there is an ache in your

chest for loneliness and your hands were never mine to hold. And they

might put me up in the sky after I die, but I will never be able to tell you

about your fire, I will never be able to kiss your constellations holy. I am a

reckoning, I am a storm, but you're a supernova drenched in tragedy.

Polaris

by Corheinne C.

Once, I heard about Polaris;

North's apple of the eye,

She stands stillshe

is constant,

As the entire Northern sky

Dances around her.

Twice, I heard about Polaris;

First in

a science class back in sophomore year,

And secondduring

my grandfather's funeral,

During his eulogy, my grandmother said,

"He was my North star," she had tears in her eyes.

I never understood Polaris.

Why she remains constant while the North sky

Revolves around her

Or why my grandmother smiles widely

When Polaris appears in the night sky.

I only understood Polaris when I met you,

"Polaris stays still while the entire north sky

Moves around it," the book says.

Polaris stays still, Polaris is constant, Polaris is always there

You are my Polaris.

clawing at floorboards

Riley Estrada (publisher)

i crack a bottle over my head.

from the floor of the bar,

i begin to bleed stars into the sky.

i bleed love as well, but you remind me,

i can't kiss you here.

people will see.

tonight is a blood moon

and my heart is full of your beat.

we dance across the shards

as you drag me home,

drunk on a cosmic joke,

and the laughing comets

grow further away.

i bed down with you

like it's my last night alive.

It's our last night together.

they are one in the same.

Stardust and Cinnamon

by Samuel Zeiberg

We are made of stars.

The same light that is in us shines down on us every time we look up into the effervescent night.

Stardust smells like cinnamon: It is heavy. Hot. It is full of eons and eons of loneliness, of light.

It's a cool summer wind at dusk,

sitting beneath an old oak tree when they start to unmask and begin their dance.

When everything stands starker and truer.

A galvanic current pulsating throughout the universe from creation to creation with a frantic gait

Searching for some port of call.

It is a maze given meaning. A portrait of nature that we as a race have thrown out who we are.

Our heroes, our desires, our needs and our deepest wants.

We glance up and say we are journeying to some far off heaven.

We are simply returning home.

The Legend of the Moon and the Sea

By Madelyn Albracht and Shanalyn Ghosh

Long ago

the moon and the sea

fell in love.

But the earth was a jealous god

and forbade their union.

To ensure this,

to keep them apart,

the earth rubbed his hands together

then breathed against them.

And the sky was created.

And the stars were born.

The earth took the moon by the scruff of the neck

and hung him in the sky.

The earth pulled the ocean towards him

and enveloped her in his arms.

Devastated

the moon collapsed

in on himself,

went quiet.

Griefstricken

the ocean carved

away at the earth,

Disfigured him.

Eons have passed

and the sea moves in waves.

The distance frightens her:

sometimes she wants to throw herself at the moon,

to explode in their love.

Other times

she wants to retreat into herself,

to nurture the parts of herself he no longer loves.

Eons have passed

and the moon turns in phases

And He feels the same way.

They are sure of one thing:

the earth wanted to keep them apart

and was successful.

We are sure of one thing:

the earth has kept them together

Maybe

by Christina Rinnerthaler

Ever since I met you, I keep writing about the stars.

I like to daydream that, *even though I don't believe people were /made/ for*
each other, when I
say "I feel like I've known you forever", maybe I'm not that wrong.

Maybe, just maybe, right after the immensity of matter exploded into what
would one day be
everything, and just before it spread and wandered and became the vastness
of space, the stardust
that would one day be you and me stuck together.

So that when you say
"I don't even remember getting to know you/ Feels like I've known you
forever"
It's because there's this tiny bit of stardust in our atoms singing to us that
maybe we are sort of
right.

i watch as you wax towards wholeness again

Riley Estrada (publisher)

i find myself living with a broken moon.

the sound of you waking from a night terror

replaces all my alarms.

i grow used to holding your craters still at night

and sleeping in the day.

we dump out the silverware drawer

and decide to eat with nothing but spoons.

they are round and soft,

like the pale skin of pluto,

and they cannot hurt you.

i tape all the black hole closets shut, when you ask.

our clothes will remain folded on the floor.

you tell me that sometimes drum beats

remind you of gunfire

so i play you my favorite symphonies

and kiss your hands.

you call me a levelheaded sun,

able to do what you are not.

rise consistently

and fall without fail.

06:30 UT.

I can see the Earth.

—*Yuri Gagarin through radio transmission to ground control during the world's first human spaceflight.*

An Educational Feature about Space Disguised as a Love Poem

by Uma Dwivedi

After Mathem Olzmann

Here's what I've got, the list of reasons why we

might work: Because we are both

supernovas wrapped in skin. Because your heart

still belongs to the milky way;

it has ever since they wrapped their nebulous arms

around your waist and kissed a galaxy into your mouth.

Because everything still tastes like stars to you.

Because you tried to swallow the ocean

just to unlearn their lips, but instead

I made you chocolate chip cookies and asked you to describe

what it's like to swallow stardust. Because, once,

I spent so long staring at a painting

my mind went into retrograde,

and you realized I loved the universe

just as much as you did. Because my heart

is a spiraling nebula that spews starlight everywhere, and I can't stop

thinking about things like the girl in a floral dress and ballet flats

riding a mountain bike I saw the other day. Because you don't mind

if I drench strangers in scattered light

as long as my heart sleeps in my own hands.

Because when you smile, the aurora borealis rips through me,

and there is so much uncoiling light I forget that shadows exist.

Because if we were both given a day to do as we pleased,

you'd try to weave the galaxy into a blanket,

and I'd smear my hands with the scent of lavender.

Because you'd wrap the sky

around both our shoulders if I looked cold.

Because you don't need words to make something beautiful.

Because, for you, the ornate chaos of the cosmos is enough,

while I'm out here trying to turn smells

into something I can run my fingers through,

because everything is electrifying in its first language

and translation is the only way to keep my atoms from overthrowing

the current. Because I'm in love with everyone I see

and you're in love with the stars, so

I listen to the 7 billion dialects

of your eyes and you find a whole night of constellations

freckled into my skin. Because this is how it's always been.

Salute

by Nikka Ursula (publisher)

Here's to the universe:

For years and years of cosmic scintillations,

For the most extensive ring pattern of the planet Saturn,

    For the 48 orbits of space travel

        by the first woman astronaut

            Valentina Tereshkova.

But also, *here's to the universe*:

For the petrichour in the morning.

For the taste of good dessert in the afternoon.

For the silent murmur of two people in the theater at night.

For the unbelievably encompassing things,

and the small handfuls we hold dear.

Here's to the universe.

(*And here's to you.*)

She is a Universe you will Never be a Part of

by efb

i want to learn the stars by name

so i can find them in the night sky when i'm alone

the universe is vast and unknowable

and i am a speck of no particular importance

but there is order in chaos

and meaning in insignificance

and if i can learn the stars by name

perhaps one will learn me, too.

A Scatter Poem about Space, Like Light Particles Escaping the Sun

by Ashton-Taylor Ackerson

The Big Bang set sail long ago,

A dense ball of heat expanding universally,

Causing intergalactic accretion and evolution,

Like a large scale Cambrian explosion,

The very same that birthed anomalocaris,

Ancient predator of the deep,

With pincers extended and mouth wide open,

Nature takes its course,

The kind of thing now seen in documentaries.

When did Animal Planet stop taping animals,

and start showcasing tree houses?

I miss Steve Irwin,

and even Jeff Corwin,

With khakis well above the knee,

Shorts that would give

the Cavaliers' color guard a run for their money.

The Planets,

Massive bodies of red and blue,

Constantly in motion,

Like band members marching drill,

Their courses always mapped out,

A fragile system relying on no collisions.

How does a black hole work?

Curving spacetime

indefinitely,

Stretching whatever's in close proximity,

It all gets sucked in,

An eternal prison of darkness,

That never comes full circle,

But what about triangle?

For many go missing in the Bermuda,

The Atlantic's black hole.

So much undiscovered,

Will things be any different,

The day the Sun begins to die?

Or will all Earth's mysterious creatures,

Shrivel up and fry?

maybe echoes don't know, which ways time can flow

by Shristi Pant (publisher)

we hear so much

about the starstuff in our veins,

but i wonder if stars had some

human in them too,

if they reached for each other,

like lost souls,

in that endless vastness.

Nebulae.
by efb

we are all

a product

of this

shipwrecked

cosmos –

driftwood

in the form

of celestial

bodies.

From the Stars to You

by Em Charny

Dear you,

It's another when space devours us whole.

When I wear the rings of Saturn as a belt,

And you cling on to the asteroid lines

Hoping it can take you home.

Dear you,

Venus looks down upon us,

Calls us cowards.

"Look at me," she says.

"Look at all I have become."

We do not speak,

We simply clutch light from the universe,

And put it in our pockets.

We say it's for safe keeping, but now

I don't know.

Dear you,

I didn't think 500,000 degrees Kelvin was that hot.

This heat, it isn't just searing,

It's suffocating,

Toxic, holy,

All above a poison to our lungs.

Why must we keep trying to let it leave?

There are lovers in the Milky Way we haven't said

Goodbye to.

Dear you,

If I could, I would call you honest.

A simple nova,

Burning at untouchable skins,

Leaving planets jealous of our light,

We tuck in pockets, too long ago.

The world is weeping into

The crevices of our skin.

Dear you,

Infinity is calling,

It tells us tenderly,

A caress of the tongue;

"I could give it all away.

All away for this."

Parallax
by Kara Joyce

Move into me.

Move into me like a rocketship reaching the atmosphere. Catch fire in my arms and let your walls be burnt away, the hard outer shell of your insecurities fading to dust in the light of open-hearted suns. Your core hurtles through the stratosphere: the solar wind and your smile blow away the things that aren't held down and you hold me down. Curious eyes twinkle down from above and watch like the sentinels of an army- how are we any different from two stars going to war? We spin closer and closer until we lose control and gravity takes control and we combine in a thousand different ways that, mathematically, should never have occurred and yet here we are: thousands of galaxies shine out from your eyes and I am both the familiar sun and the night-cold moon and we are inseparably bound now. Gravity has no reason to be so forceful and our bodies have no reason to tangle so inextricably and, yet, here we are. Orion and Cassiopeia shake hands and Sirius carries the Little Dipper by the handle and our bodies melt together like the nucleus of a soulsucked star. This is not death: this is the beginning.

Aren't we born to be phoenixes, deathless and fearless? Aren't we made of stardust? Ashes to ashes, stars collapse and create a new meaning for the word "rebirth". The universe cheers with silent emotion when two stars come together: colliding not because gravity told them to, but because even though a thousand other forces kept us in perfect orbits, a stronger force pulled my heart to yours. Newton cheered when inertia was overcome. Apples fall from trees and planets fall into black holes and you fall into me. We unite like the Big Bang never happened and our atoms were never anything but pulled so tightly together that even the constant expansion of the universe couldn't separate your hands from mine.

Your hands are solar systems in their own right- the rings of Jupiter cannot compare to the patterns of your palms and the heat of your fingertips against my skin burns like the heart of Proxima Centauri, light years away and still close enough to embrace. Constellations repeat themselves in the freckles on your skin and I trace them with the solar flare of my tongue and somewhere far away and yet very close at hand, the sun breathes out a tidal wave of wind to rip away the atmospheres left behind on stagnant planets and I breathe gently down your spine and rip away your inhibitions. Terraform this planet, my body, with your fingerprints and remind me that earthquake damage is always swept away by volcanic eruptions. Remind me that every time I shake inside, the outside is made new- old scars are wiped clean and parched, ancient oceans are replenished with lava and fury. I am a fixed system and everything that I scorch from my earth someday grows back. If I am a planet and I can stand here today in front of you and I can trace my fingers across the planes of your cheekbones, then the planes of my bones will someday hold life again.

Tectonic plates move beneath me and your hands move against me and you move into me in a way that people looking at us from far away don't see you moving at all: this lie of infinite proportions mimics the lie that our ancestors believed. Stellar parallax might have kept them from knowing how we move through our own skies and bodily parallax might keep a stranger in the night from knowing how you move against me but of one thing I have no doubt. We might live alone in the universe or we might not. Our planet might be wiped clean by a volcano or our skyscrapers might irritate the skyline forever. But of this I have no doubt-You move with me.

A Thought
by Mendy Lu

If human beings are made out of stars that have been burnt out to give us life.

And humans in turn spend their entire life, looking up at the night sky and putting wishes onto shooting stars.

Would that make us living wishes of people who lived long ago?

Never a Gentle Landing

by Nikka Ursula (publisher)

You've spend too much of your time

In a rocket ship of your own making

Zero gravity,

Everything comes easy,

You throw something in the air

And nothing gets broken.

So you let go of him

With strong confidence on your lips,

Without realizing

The heavier weight of your body

And the earth beneath your feet.

He falls, he breaks.

And captain, so do you.

You jump off high places ever since.

Selling Stars
by Katharine McCain

Bearing a basket
Dressed in green
A young girl had stars to sell
She showed off their sparkle
And "Ooo"ed at their points
Crying,
"Stars! Real stars to sell!"

(This girl was a fraud)

Hauling a hatchet
Sporting a beard
A man had need of a light
For his daughter was weeping
Afraid of the dark
Crying,
"Papa! My room must be bright!"

(A star does not banish monsters)

Lugging her skirts
Lips painted red
A woman was craving defense
Against a man in her life
His fists and his words
Crying,
Things that should never be said

(The 'shooting' in 'star' is not literal)

Toddling barefoot
Swinging his arms
A tot desired a treat
For his throat was dry
And his mouth, it yearned
Crying,
"Miss! Please, something sweet!"

(They say that stars taste of copper and dust. That if you

consume one, at an age young enough for it to matter,
you may become immortal)
(They also say you may explode)
Balancing plates
Managing drinks
Our young girl sat down to a meal
Plentiful and fine
From the magic of stars
Crying,
"Success! The fine art of a deal!"

(That night)
(Beneath a canopy of stars)
(One)
(Of four)
(Was pleased)

pluto's heart

by Shristi Pant (publisher)

sometimes humanity is a wonder in itself,

because billions of miles beyond

where we have ever tred

wasn't distance enough

for us to stop searching for meaning in this chaos,

to stop saying with shaking breath,

we see you, we see you,

are you like us too?

Supernova

by kam

i numbered my love as the stars in the sky

unnameable, unknowable

infinite

your smile was the sun

and your kisses the moon

everpresent, yet impossibly beautiful

the galaxy could not contain us, love

we were expansive, brilliant

destined

and when you left i felt that all the skies

of all the worlds

in all the universe

could not contain my grief

my heart exploding more violently than any star

my tears enough to drown this planet and all others

my pain certain to last beyond what time can measure

the stars burn out, darling, the sun will fade, the moon will fall from the sky.

when it does, how silly it will seem, to think it mattered that i loved you.

Crucible

by Savannah Stoehr

Stab yourself in the chest.

Do it with a harpoon,

because it's heavy,

and it's got a hook on the end,

and it's used to catch endangered animals.

Your chest is a chasm.

Your rib cage is an event horizon.

Don't try to pull your quarry out.

Instead, pull the whole world in.

The whole world lives inside your chest;

can you feel the shifting of the tides,

the blood of the Earth pumping for the moon?

Destroy the parts that don't matter.

Keep the silly things.

Poison smells green when it burns.

It flares up like magnesium oxidizing,

and for a split second it's blinding.

It hurts,

but better quick and gone than that other thing.

Hardly anything remains.

What remains is everything.

Feel the curve of the Milky Way in the crook of your elbow.

Feel the weatherbeaten cliffs in your eyes.

Your fingernails are all stars,

and your brain is a computer

eating up the data from a black hole.

You answer questions with questions.

It feels like sand between your toes.

The bright lights have dimmed,

and the fires have all gone out.

There's a wretched black gash where they used to be,

and it looks like a smile.

A fishhook gleams on a pile of ash.

(Beauty isn't a colorful mask;

it's bare bones in a crucible.

My fire may not burn long,

but Christ, does it burn bright.)

Sunny Smiles and Moonlit Nights

by c. abad

the first thing i learned about the universe was that i was made up of the same stuff as the sun and that mars takes six hundred eighty-seven days to go all the way around and venus only two hundred twenty-five while i only sit and i only burn, but later on i was told that we are all moving 1.3 million miles per hour standing still on this milky way star line and i finally understood how it was possible i fell so quickly for your crescent moon smile.

Andromeda

by Madelyn Albright

Will space ever seem unappealing?

Will the openness, the blackness, the lack of oxygen

ever bring me terror, instead of adventure?

Take me there. Let me try to breathe the blackness.

Let me drift into the openness that is this galaxy.

Drop me off before andromeda,

Kiss me goodbye at the first sign of the Milky Way.

Just let me feel it.

Let me feel the air leave,

the universe open and

Let me fall.

Let me forever fall.

Remember me

by kam

you think to shake loose the stars

      dormant in your blood

          for her;

but all there is to offer

is this:

      cosmic decay.

What I Mean to Say is,

I want to Flow Over Completely in Your Divinity

by efb

for a long time

kissing you has been

a way to

inhale the stardust

clogging your lungs.

planets

by ishan bose

we are the last of the circling planets

laced into the blur of a universe

not yet forgotten,

soon to lose our reluctant forms

in a soothing parade of smoke

rosebuds turn their little heads

a group of mesmerized children

to squint beyond their greenhouse veil

nestled within the fine contours of an aged moon

the unconcerned musings of others

pull me somewhere nervous,

like the morose whispers of a forest in evening

that isn't easily followed

so in this waking life of orbits and systems,

we had discovered a delicate solace in wandering—

upon the hulking, ragged backs of mountain ranges

and in slipping noiselessly to the bottom of the ocean

hearing of festoons of nebulae

that fused into cold, pearly figurines

beings of light

longing to calcify

into beings of clarity

we could strain a new path

to find what is built up

and what is turned to rust

but it takes time to ease into silence,

and even longer still to stir one's fate

summer has since dried up all our time,

and left us swirling in a stifling darkness

it is a foreign feeling,

                    to belong—

like tasting rain

                    in deep space

among the greenery and insects—

perhaps we can finally

tangle our skeletons in peace

where seasons drift off

and settle in temple pools

beyond the penumbra of your eyes

The Last Radio Transmission to Earth
by Alex Lenkei

When it came time to leave you,

outposts had been established

throughout the solar system.

There were planets for permanent habitation,

but they were farther than we'd ever been,

awash in the vast blackness of space,

and we all instinctually felt the tug

of our mother's call telling us not to wander off,

to stay where she could keep an eye on us.

When we left, we carried pieces of you with us.

We carried leaves and flowers, pressed petals

that would soon wilt and fade.

We carried pieces of tree bark to remind us

of the texture of the forest.

We carried rocks that, when pressed to our noses,

still carried the scent of centuries of earth.

We carried pinecones and fossils and

jars of soil and sand

(the dull light reflecting

off the polished grains).

We carried seashells and listened

to the song of the ocean whenever we were lonely.

All these things told stories about us,

about our past, about our first home.

The technology of the future

allowed us to carry all the old earth smells too.

We carried petrichor and lavender,

damp-forest and by-the-river.

We carried harvest-at-midnight, honey,

and sunrise-sea-salt.

After ten thousand years,

we became wanderers again, homeless nomads

seeking shelter from the night.

In those last months,

spaceships leaving almost daily,

we gathered fragments from our first home.

Out past Mars, we took one last glance homeward,

our blue marble fading away.

Perhaps you would recover without us.

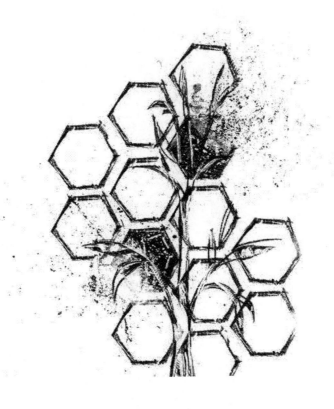

The landing took place at a preselected area in our country. I would like to tell you a little bit about what I observed.

— *Yuri Gagarin during a speech four days after his mission*

Acknowledgements

There were some lovely people involved in making this book a possibility and we couldn't have done it without all of them. Firstly, thank you to all the poets who submitted to this little project and to those who helped us out by sharing our posts. And thank you to Ada Carria for taking time to make the beautiful art to go along with the poems.

Shristi would like to thank her boyfriend Matt for all his support throughout this undertaking and her friend Samaya for always being willing to listen to her raving enthusiastically about space poetry.

Nikka Ursula would like to thank all who contributed to this work of art, those who showed enthusiasm towards this project, and those pushed it to through stratusphere through word of mouth.

Riley would like to thank her former poetry professor Sharon Cumberland for teaching her how to critique and refine her works in a way she had never before realized was possible. She would also like to thank her friend, SSP contributor, and personal poetry idol Emily Charney for setting the poetic bar extremely high and inspiring her to challenge herself. She would lastly like to thank her best friends, Abigail and Nolan, for supporting her through every endeavor, every second of the journey.

And thank you to everyone who is holding this book right now, we hope you loved reading it as much as we loved putting it together.

"We need to have people up there who can communicate what it feels like, not just pilots and engineers."
- *Buzz Aldrin, The Real Mars (2004)*

The Publishers and The Artist

Riley Estrada is a poet, musician, and future filmmaker and film major. Born in Eugene, OR, and partially raised in Western Australia, she has been writing ever since she physically knew how. Her idea of a good day is a glass of cold white wine, a Platters record, and no responsibilities whatsoever. This is her first endeavor as a publisher.

Nikka Ursula is a poet, author, and a nurse from Winnipeg, Canada. She is an enthusiast of the arts and a supporter of science, both of which meld deeply into her authored pieces. When she's not preoccupied with working as a cardiac nurse, she is knee-deep in good cinematographies and surprisingly deep Steven Universe episodes.

Shristi Pant is a poet, activist, aspiring therapist and awkward human being. Born in Nepal, she has resided in various towns in the U.S and hopes to keep traveling. When she's not helping put together super cool space poetry books, she can be found rewatching Gilmore Girls in bed for the too-embarrasing-to-count-th time.

Ada Carria is a self-taught artist who admittedly thinks more about drawing than actually drawing. There remains a stack of unused or minimally used paintbrushes and art supplies in the corner of her table. One day these will all be put to good use. In the meantime she busies herself with her second year of nursing school.

33150326R00042

Made in the USA
Middletown, DE
02 July 2016